Bookkeeping 2 Wise Guide

Level 2 Certificate in Accounting

© Michael Fardon, 2013

Image of owl © Eric Isselée-Fotolia.com

Published by Osborne Books Limited, Unit 1B Everoak Estate, Bromyard Road, Worcester WR2 5HP
Tel 01905 748071, Email books@osbornebooks.co.uk, Website www.osbornebooks.co.uk

Printed and bound by Mimeo, UK.

ISBN 978 1909173 064

how to use this Wise Guide

This Wise Guide has been designed to supplement your Tutorial and Workbook. It has two main aims:

- to reinforce your learning as you study your course
- to help you prepare for your online assessment

This Wise Guide is organised in the specific topic areas listed on pages 4 and 5. These individual topic areas have been designed to cover the main areas of study, concentrating on specific areas of difficulty. There is also an index at the back to help you find the areas you are studying or revising.

The Owl symbolises wisdom, and acts as your tutor, introducing and explaining topics. Please let us know if he is doing his job properly. If you have feedback on this material please email books@osbornebooks.co.uk

Thank you and good luck with your study and revision.

Osborne Books

REVISION TIPS

'OWL' stands for: **O**bserve **W**rite **L**earn

There are a number of well-known ways in which you can remember information:

■ *You can remember what it looks like on the page. Diagrams, lists, mindmaps, colour coding for different types of information, all help you **observe** and remember.*

■ *You can remember what you **write** down. Flash cards, post-it notes around the bathroom mirror, notes on a mobile phone all help. It is the process of writing which fixes the information in the brain.*

■ *You can **learn** by using this Wise Guide. Read through each topic carefully and then prepare your own written version on flash cards, post-it notes, wall charts – anything that you can see regularly.*

■ *Lastly, give yourself **chill out** time, your brain a chance to recover and the information time to sink in. Promise yourself treats when you have finished studying – a drink, chocolate, a work out. Relax! And pass.*

list of contents

1   Sales Ledger control account

Providing information about credit customers

When a business sells on credit to a customer it is important that there is information about its customers (trade receivables) which shows how much is owed at any one time. It is also important that this information is correct.

*A **control account** is used both as a summary of this information and also as a checking device to make sure that the accounting system is accurate.*

what exactly is a control account?

- A control account is a 'master' account which provides information about a number of individual accounts which are known as 'subsidiary' accounts.

- The **Sales Ledger control account** is a 'master' account which 'controls' subsidiary accounts for each of its credit customers (trade receivables).

- The **Sales Ledger control account** records the **totals** of different types of transactions – eg sales, sales returns, bank receipts – in the subsidiary accounts.

Sales Ledger control account as master account

Sales Ledger Control Account	
totals of:	**totals of:**
Balances b/d	Bank (receipts)
Credit sales	Sales returns
Returned cheques	Settlement discount allowed
	Irrecoverable debts
	Balances c/d

SALES LEDGER
customer subsidiary accounts

Atlas Limited	
Balance b/d	Bank receipts
Sales	Sales returns
	Balance c/d

Bartro Limited	
Balance b/d	Bank receipts
Sales	Sales returns
	Balance c/d

Celia Limited	
Balance b/d	Bank receipts
Sales	Discount all'wd
	Balance c/d

Delia Limited	
Balance b/d	Bank receipts
Sales	Sales returns
Returned cheque	Balance c/d

Note about double-entry

Sales Ledger control account is a double-entry account in the General Ledger. The entries in the customer Sales Ledger subsidiary accounts **are not part of the double-entry system**.

The entries in the control account and the subsidiary accounts are on the **same side**.

what are the entries in the Sales Ledger control account?

Sales Ledger Control Account			
Dr			**Cr**
Balance b/d	10,000	**Bank**	15,000
total customer balances brought down		*total receipts from credit customers*	
Credit sales	19,500	**Credit sales returns**	480
total credit sales to customers		*total sales returns from customers*	
Returned cheques	500	**Settlement discount allowed**	195
dishonoured (bounced) cheques issued by customers		*total settlement discount allowed*	
		Irrecoverable debts	900
		total irrecoverable debts written off	
total customer balances at end of period		**Balance c/d**	13,425
	30,000		30,000
Balance b/d	13,425		

where in the accounting system do the entries come from?

Sales Ledger Control Account			
Dr			**Cr**
Balance b/d	10,000	**Bank**	15,000
balance of the account brought down		*cash book receipts*	
Credit sales	19,500	**Credit sales returns**	480
sales day book total (including VAT)		*sales returns day book total (inc. VAT)*	
Returned cheques	500	**Settlement discount allowed**	195
cash book, credit side (cheques deducted by the bank)		*cash book discount all'wd column total*	
		Irrecoverable debts	900
		irrecoverable debts written off account	
balance of account carried down		**Balance c/d**	13,425
	30,000		30,000
Balance b/d	13,425		

reconciling the control account with the subsidiary accounts

The Sales Ledger control account is a useful way of checking the accuracy of the balances in the Sales Ledger subsidiary accounts.

The process is as follows (using the example on the previous page, with figures):

- The subsidiary customer accounts are balanced at regular intervals. The balance b/d (brought down) in each case will be a **debit** in normal circumstances.
- The Sales Ledger control account is balanced at the same time and the balance brought down on the **debit** side. The balance in this case is £1,277.85.
- The subsidiary customer account balances are listed on a schedule and totalled:

BALANCES OF TRADE RECEIVABLES at 2 April 20XX	
Atlas Limited	£350.50
Bartro Limited	£630.40
Celia Limited	£126.95
Delia Limited	£170.00
TOTAL	£1,277.85

- The customer accounts total and the Sales Ledger control account balance agree. The figure is £1,277.85.
- There are no errors or discrepancies in the bookkeeping.

possible discrepancies in the reconciliation

When reconciling the total credit customer balances (trade receivables) with the Sales Ledger control account final balance you need to be aware of the types of discrepancy that can occur.

When faced with a difference you will need to work out the amount of the difference and establish which total is the higher.

The differences can result from:
- wrong figures entered (too high or too low)
- figures omitted
- figures entered twice
- figures entered on the wrong side of an account

managing customer accounts – irrecoverable debts

- A well-run business will keep a careful eye on the balances of its customers in its Sales Ledger.

- If any customer who buys on credit goes 'bust' the seller is likely to be left with a customer debt in its Sales Ledger which it is unlikely to be able to recover. This is known as an **irrecoverable debt**.

- As an irrecoverable debt represents a loss to the business it will have to be written off in the accounts and eventually deducted from profit:
  - debit **Irrecoverable debts written off account**
  - credit **Sales Ledger control account** (and customer subsidiary account)

managing customer accounts – aged receivables analysis

- One way in which a business can monitor its customer balances is by using an **aged receivables analysis**.

- This is a regular management report which sets out each customer, what they owe and for what time periods their debts have been outstanding. See the next page for an extract of this analysis showing a sample of four customers.

Sabrina Limited Aged receivables analysis as at 30 June 20XX				
Customer	**Total**	**0-30 days**	**31-60 days**	**61+ days**
	£	£	£	£
Atlas Ltd	3,510	0	0	3,510
Bartro Ltd	1,840	1,620	220	0
Celia Ltd	760	760	0	0
Delia Ltd	2,330	330	2,000	0
Totals	8,440	2,710	2,220	3,510

Customer list

Total balance outstanding of each customer

Amounts outstanding up to 30 days

Amounts outstanding from 31 to 60 days

Amounts outstanding for 61 days or more
The £3,510 owed by Atlas Ltd will need chasing up!

2   Purchases Ledger control account

Providing information about credit purchases

When a business buys on credit from suppliers (trade payables) it is important that the business knows how much is owed at any one time, and that it pays on time. It is very important that this information is accurate.

*A **control account** is used both as a summary of this information and also as a checking device to make sure that the accounting system is accurate.*

what exactly is a control account?

- A control account is a 'master' account which provides information about a number of individual accounts which are known as 'subsidiary' accounts.

- The **Purchases Ledger control account** is a 'master' account which 'controls' individual 'subsidiary' accounts for each of its suppliers (trade payables).

- The **Purchases Ledger control account** records the **totals** of types of transaction – eg purchases, purchases returns, bank payments – in the subsidiary accounts.

Purchases Ledger control account as master account

Purchases Ledger Control Account	
totals of:	**totals of:**
Bank (payments)	Balances b/d
Purchases returns	Credit purchases
Settlement discount received	
Balances c/d	

Note about double-entry

Purchases Ledger control account is a double-entry account in the General Ledger. The entries in the supplier Purchases Ledger subsidiary accounts **are not part of the double-entry system**.

The entries in the control account and the subsidiary accounts are on the **same side**.

PURCHASES LEDGER supplier subsidiary accounts

Allora Limited	
Bank payments	Balance b/d
Purchases returns	Purchases
Balance c/d	

Bella Limited	
Bank payments	Balance b/d
Purchases returns	Purchases
Balance c/d	

Centro Limited	
Bank payments	Balance b/d
Discount received	Purchases
Balance c/d	

Dritto Limited	
Bank payments	Balance b/d
Purchases returns	Purchases
Balance c/d	

what are the entries in the Purchases Ledger control account?

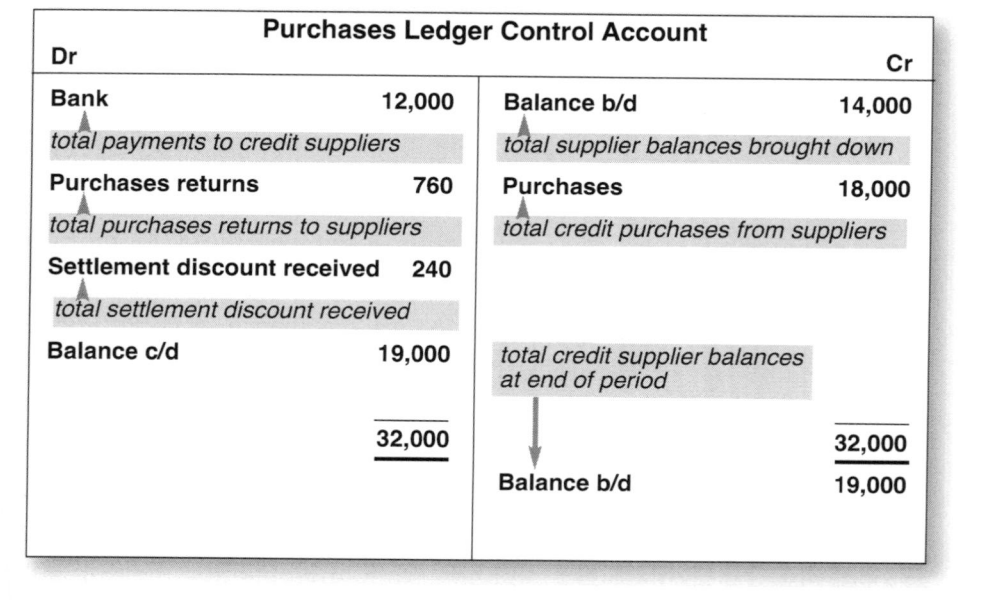

Purchases Ledger Control Account			
Dr			**Cr**
Bank	12,000	**Balance b/d**	14,000
total payments to credit suppliers		*total supplier balances brought down*	
Purchases returns	760	**Purchases**	18,000
total purchases returns to suppliers		*total credit purchases from suppliers*	
Settlement discount received	240		
total settlement discount received			
Balance c/d	19,000	*total credit supplier balances at end of period*	
	32,000		32,000
		Balance b/d	19,000

where in the accounting system do the entries come from?

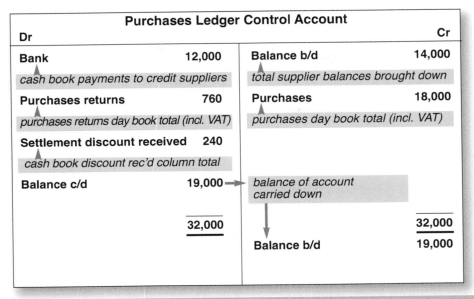

Purchases Ledger Control Account			
Dr			**Cr**
Bank	12,000	**Balance b/d**	14,000
cash book payments to credit suppliers		*total supplier balances brought down*	
Purchases returns	760	**Purchases**	18,000
purchases returns day book total (incl. VAT)		*purchases day book total (incl. VAT)*	
Settlement discount received	240		
cash book discount rec'd column total			
Balance c/d	19,000	*balance of account carried down*	
	32,000		32,000
		Balance b/d	19,000

reconciling the control account with the subsidiary accounts

The Purchases Ledger control account is a useful way of checking the accuracy of the balances in the Purchases Ledger subsidiary accounts.

The process is as follows (using the example on the previous page, with figures):

- The subsidiary supplier accounts are balanced at regular intervals. The balance b/d (brought down) in each case will be a **credit** in normal circumstances.

- The Purchases Ledger control account is balanced at the same time and the balance brought down on the **credit** side. The balance in this case is £1,585.72.

- The subsidiary supplier account balances are listed on a schedule and totalled:

BALANCES OF TRADE PAYABLES at 2 April 20XX	
Allora Limited	£237.50
Bella Limited	£762.95
Centro Limited	£275.30
Dritto Limited	£309.97
TOTAL	£1,585.72

- The supplier accounts total and the Purchases Ledger control account balance agree. The figure is £1,585.72.
- There are no errors or discrepancies in the bookkeeping.

possible discrepancies in the reconciliation

When reconciling the total credit supplier balances (trade payables) with the Purchases Ledger control account final balance you need to be aware of the types of discrepancy that can occur.

When faced with a difference you will need to work out the amount of the difference and establish which total is the higher.

The differences can result from:

- wrong figures entered (too high or too low)
- figures omitted
- figures entered twice
- figures entered on the wrong side of an account

Collecting accounting data for the VAT Return

VAT is a tax on sales and an important money earner for the UK Government. All except the smallest businesses need to register for VAT.

A business needs to keep detailed and accurate accounting records and totals of VAT it pays on what it buys and VAT it charges on what it sells.

The difference between these two figures is the amount that has to be settled with HMRC.

A business will therefore need to complete a VAT Return on a regular basis to work out the amount it will either pay to – or claim back from – the tax office.

*A **VAT control account** collects all this information together and calculates the amount of VAT due. An example of the account format is shown on the next page.*

accounting records (books of prime entry) → VAT CONTROL ACCOUNT (General Ledger) → online VAT Return (VAT paid or claimed back online)

EXAMPLE: VAT Control Account

Dr	input VAT	**VAT Control Account**	output VAT	Cr
Purchases		20,000	Sales	30,000
Sales returns		3,000	Purchases returns	4,500
Cash purchases		5,000	Cash sales	6,500
Petty cash		16		
VAT on irrecoverable debts		124		
Balance b/d		12,860	output VAT due to HMRC	
		41,000		41,000
			Balance b/d	12,860

input VAT and output VAT

■ VAT paid by a business on its purchases – **input VAT** – can be claimed back from HMRC

■ VAT charged by a business on its sales – **output VAT** – has to be paid to HMRC

■ the difference between **output VAT** and **input VAT** is the amount **paid to** HMRC

■ but . . if input VAT is greater than output VAT the net amount will be **claimed from** HMRC

what are the debit entries in the VAT control account?

VAT Control Account extract (debit side)	
Purchases	20,000
Sales returns	3,000
Cash purchases	5,000
Petty cash	16
VAT on irrecoverable debts	124
Balance c/d	12,860
	41,000

Purchases Day Book, VAT column total – VAT paid on credit purchase invoices.

Sales Returns Day Book, VAT column total – VAT allowed on credit notes to customers.

Cash Book – VAT column total of VAT paid on cash purchases.

Petty Cash Book – VAT column total of VAT paid on petty cash purchases.

VAT previously paid to HMRC but now part of a **irrecoverable debt written off**. HMRC allows this VAT to be claimed back by the seller.

Balance carried down onto credit side of the account – **VAT due to be paid to HMRC**. It is a liability and so will be a credit balance.

what are the credit entries in the VAT control account?

VAT Control Account extract (credit side)	
Sales	30,000
Purchases returns	4,500
Cash sales	6,500
	41,000
Balance b/d	12,860

Sales Day Book, VAT column total – VAT charged on credit sales invoices.

Purchases Returns Day Book, VAT column total – VAT on credit notes from suppliers.

Cash Book – VAT column total of VAT paid on cash sales.

Balance brought down on credit side of the account – **VAT due to be paid to HMRC**. It is a liability and therefore a credit balance.

If the balance had been brought down on the debit side it would have been VAT owed by HMRC and therefore an asset.

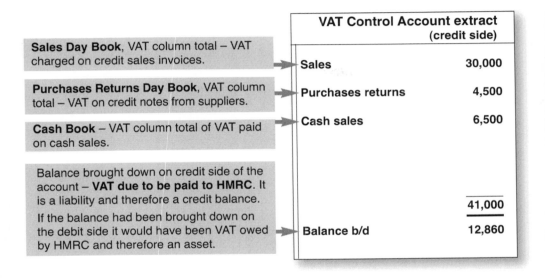

VAT control account – checking the amount due – payment or refund?

It is important to check the balance of the VAT control account against the amount of VAT entered on the VAT Return:

- Is the amount of VAT calculated correct? In other words, is the 'balance b/d' the same as the amount entered on the VAT Return (Box 5)?
- Confirm whether it is a VAT payment to make, or a VAT refund to claim. Remember:

VAT that you have paid on your purchases/expenses (input tax) = VAT you can reclaim.

VAT on sales you have made (output tax) = VAT you have to pay to HMRC.

If output (sales) VAT is greater than input (purchases) VAT, you will need to make a payment.

If output (sales) VAT is less than input (purchases) VAT, you will need to claim for a refund of VAT.

A credit balance on VAT control account means you have to make a payment.

A debit balance on VAT control account means you have to claim for a refund.

VAT control account – a summary

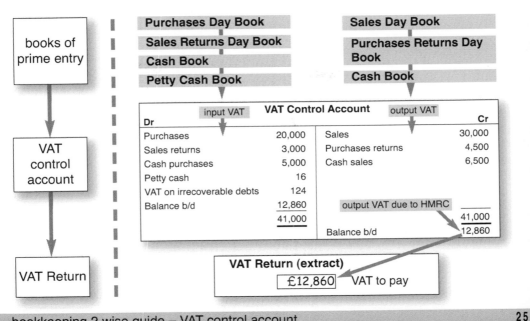

books of prime entry		

Purchases Day Book
Sales Returns Day Book
Cash Book
Petty Cash Book

Sales Day Book
Purchases Returns Day Book
Cash Book

VAT Control Account

input VAT → | output VAT →

Dr			Cr	
Purchases	20,000	Sales	30,000
Sales returns	3,000	Purchases returns	4,500
Cash purchases	5,000	Cash sales	6,500
Petty cash	16		
VAT on irrecoverable debts	124	output VAT due to HMRC	
Balance b/d	12,860		41,000
	41,000	Balance b/d	12,860

VAT control account

VAT Return (extract)

£12,860 VAT to pay

VAT Return

Books of prime entry – the role of the journal

*In any accounting system it is important that any transaction has a formal starting point in the accounting records – in a **book of prime entry**.*

***Day books** for sales and purchases are **books of prime entry** and are written up from documents such as invoices and credit notes. The figures from these documents are listed and used as the source of the double-entry.*

But there are other transactions which do not involve a formal document, eg an irrecoverable debt written off, an error in the accounts, notified by email. These will need to be recorded formally so that the double-entry can be carried out accurately and in an organised way. This is done in a **book of prime entry** called the **journal**.

definition of the journal

- The journal is the book of prime entry for accounting transactions not catered for in the other routinely used books of prime entry, eg the day books.

- The journal lists transactions so that they can be entered in the double-entry accounts in the General Ledger.

use of the journal

- The journal can be used for transactions such as:
  - setting up the opening (first) entries in a set of accounts for a new business
  - writing off irrecoverable debts
  - writing up the double-entry accounts for payroll transactions (wages, salaries, tax)
  - correcting errors in the accounting system

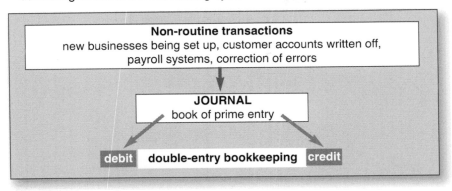

Non-routine transactions
new businesses being set up, customer accounts written off,
payroll systems, correction of errors

JOURNAL
book of prime entry

debit **double-entry bookkeeping** credit

format of the journal

The journal format is set out as follows:

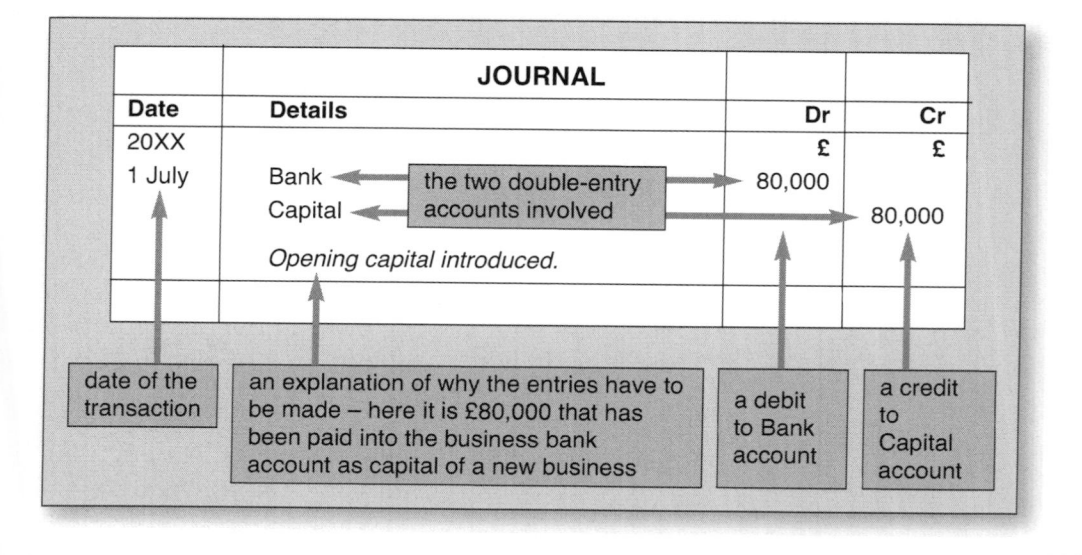

notes on the format of the journal

■ The account names are shown in the Details column and the debit entry is listed first.

■ The explanation which follows the account names is the reason for the journal entry.

■ There are columns for the required debit and credit entries.

■ The debit column is to the left and the credit column is to the right.

■ The debit and credit columns should always balance (ie have the same total).

■ Each entry is ruled off at the bottom to separate it from the next entry.

■ There may be more than two account entries in a transaction, but the debit and credit entries must always balance, as in this irrecoverable debt write off:

Date	Details	Dr	Cr
20XX		£	£
30 June	Irrecoverable debts written off	800.00	
	VAT	160.00	
	Sales Ledger control		960.00
	Irrecoverable debt written off.	960.00	960.00

Setting up a new accounting system

There will be times when a new accounting system will have to be set up from scratch, for example when a business starts up for the first time. In cases like these there are no existing double-entry accounts and the journal will be the book of prime entry to generate entries for the accounts.

It is quite possible that the business may have been trading already and there will be existing totals for sales and purchases and money in the bank to account for.

opening journal entries – debit or credit?

If you are opening up a set of accounts for the first time you are likely to be faced with a list of figures for assets, liabilities, capital, VAT, purchases and sales, but with **no indication of whether they are debits or credits**. You will need to be able to work out which they are in order to post your journal entries and get the debits and credits to balance. Just like a Trial Balance! You should try to memorise the list on the next page.

debits	credits
Bank account (cash at bank)	Bank overdraft
Property	Capital
Vehicles	Bank loan
Expenses items	Income items
Purchases	Sales
VAT on purchases	VAT on sales
Sales Ledger control account	Purchases Ledger control account
TOTAL DEBITS ← *equals* →	TOTAL CREDITS

Debits =
- Assets
- Bank (cash in the bank)
- Purchases and expenses
- VAT on purchases
- Sales Ledger control account

Credits =
- Liabilities and capital
- Bank overdraft and loans
- Sales and income
- VAT on sales
- Purchases Ledger control account

EXAMPLE: Journal for opening entries

You have just started in business and have been trading for a month.

You have kept accurate accounting records but have not yet set up a double-entry system. Your accountant has suggested that you:

- enter all the following amounts in a journal
- make sure that the journal balances (ie the debit and credit totals agree)
- set up the double-entry accounts

The amounts to enter are:

	£
Bank (cash at bank)	1,490
Purchases	10,500
Sales	12,000
Inventory	5,000
Computer equipment	12,500
Capital	17,490

The journal will look like this:

Date	Details	Dr	Cr
20XX		£	£
1 July	Bank (cash at bank)	1,490	
	Purchases	10,500	
	Inventory	5,000	
	Computer equipment	12,500	
	Sales		12,000
	Capital		17,490
		29,490	29,490
	Opening entries at start of business		

Note that:

- the debits are entered first and the credits last
- the total of the debits and the total of the credits agree
- double-entry accounts can now be set up and the debits and credits posted to them

6   Journals – irrecoverable debts

Writing off irrecoverable debts

*A business will sometimes encounter the situation where a customer debt becomes **irrecoverable** – in other words, despite all its efforts in trying to get the money back, the customer will not, or cannot, repay it.*

The debt will be recorded in the customer account in the Sales Ledger and is likely also to include VAT charged to the customer. This will need to be 'written off' – ie taken out of the Sales Ledger as a loss to the business.

the process of writing off an irrecoverable debt

The accounting entries needed are:

debit	Irrecoverable debts written off account
debit	VAT account
credit	Sales Ledger control account (and the customer subsidiary account)

This is set up by a **journal entry (prime entry)**, usually authorised by a managerial email (which will be attached to the journal as evidence of the transaction).

EXAMPLE: Apex Glazing's account written off as an irrecoverable debt

Date	Details	Dr	Cr
20XX		£	£
31 May	Irrecoverable debts written off	200	
	VAT	40	
	Sales Ledger control		240
		240	240
	Balance of Apex Glazing's Sales Ledger account written off as an irrecoverable debt, authorised by email from S Tingi, Accounts Manager.		

Note that:

- the debt of £240 is split into the sales amount (£200) and the VAT (£40)
- the debits come before the credit and the totals balance
- the narrative quotes the email authorisation for the transaction

7 Journals – payroll transactions

processing the payroll

Processing the payroll is a complicated procedure. The employer has to pay the employees and also needs to calculate and make all the deductions for tax, National Insurance, pension contributions and voluntary contributions to various bodies.

*The solution is to use a Wages control account to record all the various transactions which are originated in the **journal** – the book of prime entry.*

what are the transactions?

The payments you need to remember are listed here and on the next page – they should be memorised:

- **gross pay** – the amount of pay before any deductions, eg tax, are made

- **net pay** – the amount which employees actually receive after deductions

- **income tax** – the amount of tax deducted from employees' gross pay and paid to HMRC

- **National Insurance Contributions** – there are two amounts which the employer has to pay direct to HMRC:
  - the **employer's** National Insurance Contributions (NIC), an expense to the employer
  - the **employees'** National Insurance Contributions (NIC) deducted from employees' gross pay by the employer

- **Pension Contributions** – there are often two amounts which the employer has to pay direct to the pension provider:
  - the **employer's** pension contributions, ie pension contributions for the employees provided by the employer
  - the **employees'** pension contributions, deducted from employees' pay by the employer

- **Voluntary deductions** – amounts deducted from pay by the employer at the employee's request, eg Trade Union subscriptions, charitable donations

This is all illustrated in the diagram on the next page.

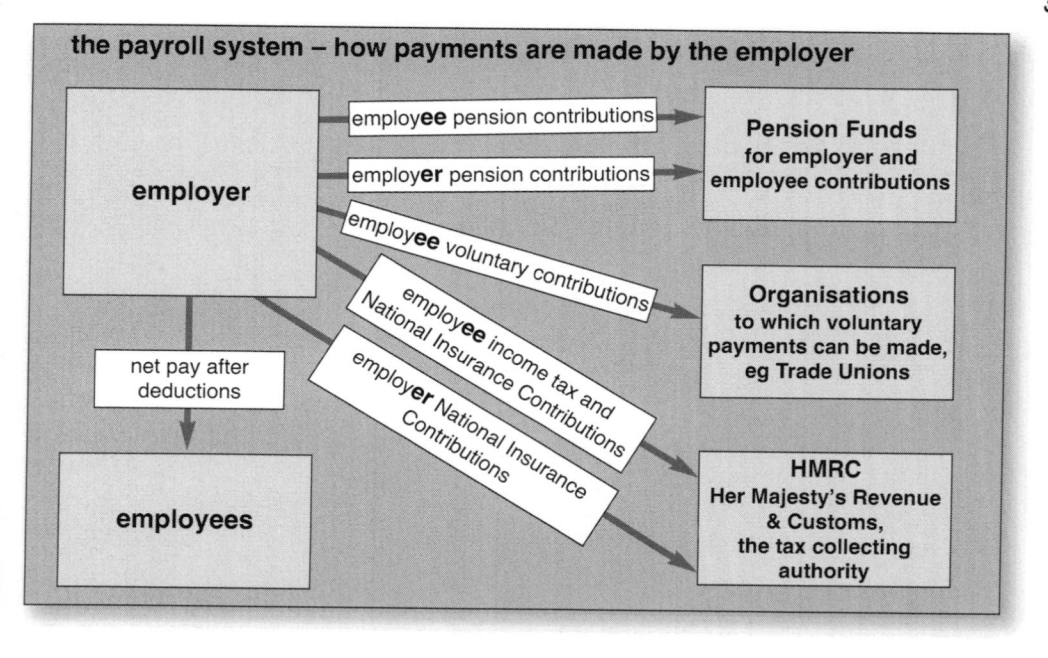

Wages control account

- All accounting entries relating to payroll pass through the **Wages control account**, which is written up from entries in the journal.

- The Wages control account is a proper double-entry account: a debit or credit to Wages control account will be a credit or debit in one of the other payroll accounts.

what do the other payroll accounts record?

Bank	– payment of net pay to employees
	– payments to HMRC of tax and National Insurance, pension funds, voluntary deductions
Wages expense	– the payroll expense to the employer, ie . . .
	– employees' gross pay
	– employer's National Insurance Contributions (NIC)
	– any employer's pension or other contributions
HM Revenue & Customs	– amounts due to HM Revenue & Customs for income tax and National Insurance Contributions (NIC)
Pension funds	– contributions from both employer and employees

EXAMPLE: Wages Control Account

Wages Control Account			
Dr			**Cr**
Bank	26,000	Wages expense	39,910
HM Revenue & Customs	10,000		
Pension fund	3,670		
Trade Union subscriptions	240	these totals will equal each other, leaving a nil balance, and no balance to bring down	
	39,910		39,910

Note that normal double-entry rules apply to Wages control account:

- All debit entries in the **Wages control account** will require a credit entry in the 'other' account, for example a credit of £26,000 to Bank account for the wages paid.

- All credit entries in the **Wages control account** will require a debit entry in the 'other' account, for example a debit of £39,910 to Wages expense account.

how the journal fits into the payroll process

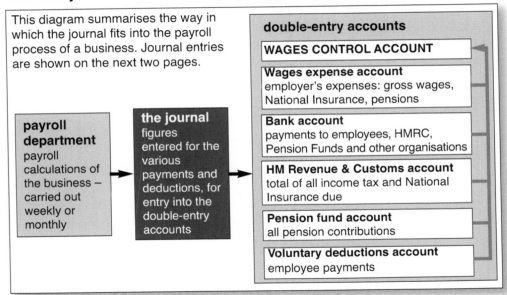

This diagram summarises the way in which the journal fits into the payroll process of a business. Journal entries are shown on the next two pages.

payroll department
payroll calculations of the business – carried out weekly or monthly

the journal
figures entered for the various payments and deductions, for entry into the double-entry accounts

double-entry accounts

WAGES CONTROL ACCOUNT

Wages expense account
employer's expenses: gross wages, National Insurance, pensions

Bank account
payments to employees, HMRC, Pension Funds and other organisations

HM Revenue & Customs account
total of all income tax and National Insurance due

Pension fund account
all pension contributions

Voluntary deductions account
employee payments

journal entries needed for processing payroll

These are the journal entries for the Wages control account on page 40. Note that:

■ Each journal entry involves a posting to Wages control account.

■ The 'other' account posted, follows double-entry rules, for example Wages expense is a debit (an expense) and the other accounts are credits – bank payment and liabilities amounts owed.

Date	Details	Dr	Cr
20XX		£	£
30 June	Wages expense	39,910	
	Wages control		39,910
	transfer of wages expense		

Date	Details	Dr	Cr
20XX		£	£
30 June	Wages control	26,000	
	Bank		26,000
	net wages paid to employees		

Date	Details	Dr	Cr
20XX		£	£
30 June	Wages control	10,000	
	HM Revenue & Customs		10,000
	amount due to HM Revenue & Customs		

Date	Details	Dr	Cr
20XX		£	£
30 June	Wages control	3,670	
	Pension fund		3,670
	amount due to Pension fund		

Date	Details	Dr	Cr
20XX		£	£
30 June	Wages control	240	
	Trade Union fees		240
	amount due for Trade Union subscriptions		

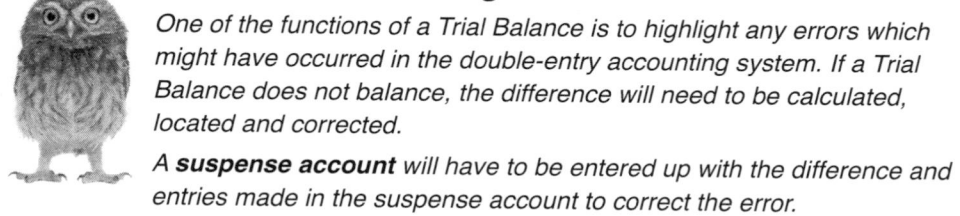

sorting out accounting errors

One of the functions of a Trial Balance is to highlight any errors which might have occurred in the double-entry accounting system. If a Trial Balance does not balance, the difference will need to be calculated, located and corrected.

*A **suspense account** will have to be entered up with the difference and entries made in the suspense account to correct the error.*

*All these correcting transactions will be originated using the **journal**.*

*But there are sometimes errors which do **not** show up in a Trial Balance and these will also need to be corrected through the **journal**.*

So, when dealing with errors the important thing you have to do is to decide if it is:

- ▨ *an error **not revealed** by the Trial Balance – no suspense account needed*
- ▨ *an error **revealed** by the Trial Balance – you will need a suspense account*

setting up the suspense account

▪ If the Trial Balance totals show a difference, **calculate** the difference, eg £300.

▪ Identify **which side** – debit or credit – has the higher total.

▪ If the **credit** side of the Trial Balance has the higher total, post the figure to the **debit** side of suspense account . . .

Dr	Suspense account (credit side of Trial Balance greater)				Cr
		£			£
31 Dec	Trial balance difference	300			

▪ If the **debit** side of the Trial Balance has the higher total, post the figure to the **credit** side of suspense account . . .

Dr	Suspense account (debit side of Trial Balance greater)				Cr
		£			£
			31 Dec	Trial balance difference	300

six errors <u>not</u> revealed by the Trial Balance (no suspense account)

▨ **error of omission** – a transaction has not been entered at all

▨ **error of commission** – a transaction has been entered in the wrong person's account, eg the wrong customer has been invoiced

▨ **error of principle** – a transaction has been entered in the wrong type of account, eg fuel for a vehicle (an expense) has been entered into vehicles account (an asset account)

▨ **error of original entry** – a transaction has been entered using the same figure as both debit and credit, but using the wrong figure

▨ **reversal of entries** – the same figure has been entered but on the wrong side of both accounts involved

▨ **compensating error** – two separate errors cancel each other out, for example:
  – an overstatement **and** understatement of £50 on the same side, or
  – positive or negative errors on both sides, eg + £50 **or** – £50 on both sides

six errors revealed by the Trial Balance (suspense account needed)

If the balances of the debit and credit columns of the Trial Balance do not agree, you should set up a suspense account with the difference – on the correct side. You will then use that figure and look for the error. It could be caused by any of the following:

■ **calculation errors in accounts** – eg an error when adding up figures and balancing a ledger account

■ **single entry transactions** – eg entering a debit but forgetting to enter the credit

■ **using two debits or two credits** – eg debiting Insurance account and also debiting Bank account (which should have had a credit entry)

■ **using different amounts on the debits and credits** – eg reversing figures such as a £23 (debit) and £32 (credit)

■ **error in transferring account balance to the Trial Balance** – simply entering a wrong figure in the Trial Balance, eg entering a balance of £5,500 instead of £5,550

■ **omitting a General Ledger account in the Trial Balance** – leaving an account balance out of the Trial Balance completely

EXAMPLES: journals for correction of errors

error of omission not revealed on Trial Balance

Credit purchase of £480 including VAT on invoice 28374 from J R Supplies omitted from the accounting system. Invoice located having slipped behind filing cabinet.

The journal is the book of prime entry for entering the transaction into the accounting system.

Date	Details	Dr	Cr
20XX		£	£
30 June	Purchases	400.00	
	VAT	80.00	
	Purchases Ledger control		480.00
		480.00	480.00
	Invoice 28374 omitted from accounts.		
	Purchases Ledger: credit J R Supplies		

Note: a credit entry for £480 would be made in J R Supplies' Purchases Ledger 'subsidiary account'.

EXAMPLE: error of principle not revealed on Trial Balance

The cost of property maintenance, £245 (no VAT), cash receipt 452, was debited to Property account (asset account) instead of Property maintenance account (expense account).

The journal (a book of prime entry) sets up the transfer of the £245 from Property account to Property maintenance account.

The credit to Property account cancels out the original incorrect debit for the same amount.

Date	Details	Dr	Cr
20XX		£	£
30 June	Property maintenance account	245.00	
	Property account		245.00
	Correction of posting error, receipt 452		

EXAMPLE: calculation error revealed by the Trial Balance

*The Trial Balance does not balance; the debit side is £50 higher than the credit side. There has been a calculation error of £50 in the Sales account which is £50 lower than it should be. £50 has been posted as a **credit** to Suspense account.*

You will need to cancel out the error and remove the £50 from the Suspense account. The journal entry is as follows:

Date	Details	Dr	Cr
20XX		£	£
30 June	Suspense	50.00	
	Sales		50.00
	Correction of undercasting of sales by £50		

double-entry needed:

Debit   **Suspense account** £50 (this entry cancels out the original credit for £50 and brings Suspense account to a zero balance).

Credit   **Sales account** £50 (this entry increases the balance of Sales account by £50 and brings it up to the correct balance).

EXAMPLE: single entry error revealed by the Trial Balance

*The Trial Balance does not balance; the **credit** side is £150 **higher** than the debit side. We have made a £150 payment to Arthur Clack, a supplier, to close his account but have forgotten to make the debit entry to the account which remains open. £150 has been posted as a **debit** to Suspense account.*

You will need to cancel out the error and remove the £150 debit balance from the Suspense account by debiting the supplier account. The journal entry is as follows:

Date	Details	Dr	Cr
20XX		£	£
30 June	Arthur Clack	150.00	
	Suspense		150.00
	Correction of error – account closure		

double-entry needed:

Debit **Arthur Clack account** £150 to close the account

Credit **Suspense account** £150 to bring balance to zero

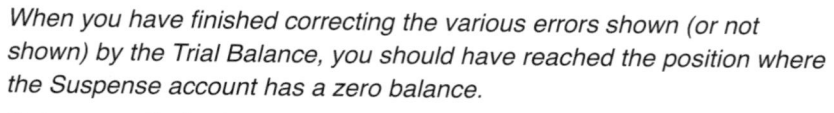

correcting the Trial Balance

When you have finished correcting the various errors shown (or not shown) by the Trial Balance, you should have reached the position where the Suspense account has a zero balance.

But you are likely also to have changed the balances of some of the accounts which make up the Trial Balance.

*So you will have to **redraft the Trial Balance** and total the columns again, with the result that the total of the debit balances should now equal the total of the credit balances.*

redrafting the Trial Balance – debits and credits – some revision

You may already have studied the principles underlying on which side of a Trial Balance each balance should be entered. If you have, this is a useful opportunity for revision.

On the next page are some hints on which side of a Trial Balance each entry should go.

debit or credit?

- In an exam situation you are likely to be given a list of balances but you will not be told whether each figure is a debit or a credit.

- The problem here, of course, is deciding between debit or credit.

- The rules are straightforward and can be remembered by the two words:

  DEAD (for the **debits**)   **CLIC** (for the **credits**)

These words stand for the types of account listed in the Trial Balance:

D ebit balances	**C** redit balances
E xpenses	**L** iabilities
A ssets	**I** ncome
D rawings	**C** apital

'DEAD CLIC' is just one way of helping you to remember your debits and credits. Your tutor may suggest other ways. The important thing is to remember the principles behind debits and credits.

10 Banks and Building Societies

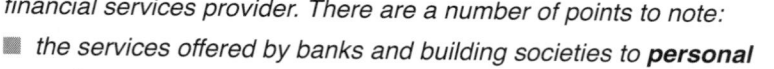

the main problem – what is the difference?

*You are often asked to describe the financial services offered by banks and building societies and to **identify the differences** between the two types of financial services provider. There are a number of points to note:*

■ *the services offered by banks and building societies to **personal** customers are very similar*

■ *all banks offer services to **businesses** but only the very large building societies deal with businesses. The smaller mutual societies deal only with personal customers.*

But banks and building societies are set up very differently . . .

banks and building societies – definitions

■ **bank**   a bank is a **limited company**, owned by **shareholders**, for example Lloyds TSB, RBS, HSBC, Barclays, Halifax, Santander

■ **building society**   a building society is a **mutual organisation**, owned by its **members** (ie its customers), eg Yorkshire Building Society

financial services availability from banks and building societies

financial services for personal and business customers	available from banks	available from <u>smaller</u> building societies
▦ personal current accounts	✔	✔
▦ personal savings and investments	✔	✔
▦ personal overdrafts and loans	✔	✔
▦ personal debit and credit cards	✔	✔
▦ house mortgages	✔	✔
▦ personal insurance	✔	✔
▦ travel money	✔	✔
▦ safe custody	✔	
▦ wills and trusts	✔	
▦ business current accounts	✔	
▦ business loans and finance	✔	
▦ business investment accounts	✔	
▦ business debit & credit cards	✔	

11 Payment systems

payment systems – old and new

There are many different ways of making payment, some centuries old and slow (eg the cheque) and some relatively new and much quicker (eg the Faster Payments Service).

In your studies you will need to identify all the main types of payment and know which is most appropriate to each situation.

methods of payment

The main forms of making payment (other than cash) are:

- cheque
- debit card
- BACS – direct credit
- BACS – direct debit
- CHAPS
- bank giro credit
- credit card
- BACS – standing order
- Faster Payments Service
- Bank draft

cheque

- a paper-based form of payment which has been in operation for over 350 years
- a cheque has to be paid in at a bank and sent to the bank of the person who issued it for payment
- payment can be refused by the issuer's bank (the cheque may be 'dishonoured')
- a cheque is subject to the '2-4-6' clearing cycle: after **2** days, **interest** can be paid on the cheque amount; after **4** days the cheque amount can be **withdrawn** from the account; after **6** days the cheque can be assumed to be '**paid**'

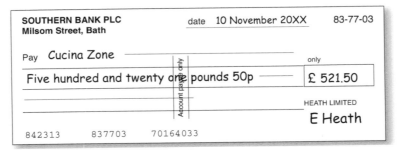

| SOUTHERN BANK PLC | date 10 November 20XX | 83-77-03 |
| Milsom Street, Bath | | |

Pay Cucina Zone ———————————————————— only

Five hundred and twenty one pounds 50p ———— £ 521.50

Account payee only

HEATH LIMITED

E Heath

842313   837703   70164033

bank giro credit

- ▓ a bank giro credit (or paying-in slip) is a **paper slip** which is paid in with a cheque (or cash) at a bank, either for an account at that branch or an account at another bank
- ▓ the bank giro credit is often used for paying utility (eg gas or electricity) bills – it forms the tear-off slip at the bottom of the bill
- ▓ the clearance time is three working days

debit card

- ▓ a plastic card used for making purchases at the counter, by telephone or online
- ▓ the money is taken out **electronically** from the purchaser's **bank account** normally within two days of the purchase, depending on the place or method of purchase

credit card

- ▓ a plastic card used for making purchases at the counter, by telephone or online
- ▓ the money is added on **electronically** to the purchaser's **credit card account**
- ▓ the customer pays the credit card company after the monthly statement arrives

BACS (Bankers Automated Clearing Services)

- a computer payment transfer system owned and operated by the banks
- payment is set up electronically and is transferred electronically from bank account to bank account
- the clearing cycle is normally three days
- there are three main types of BACS transfer: direct credit, direct debit, standing order:

direct credits	direct debits	standing orders
– regular bulk payments	– variable amounts	– regular payments
– variable amounts	– variable timing	– regular amounts
– 3 day payment cycle	– 3 day payment cycle	– 3 day payment cycle
– set up by business sending the money	– set up by business receiving the money	– set up by person sending the money
used for:	used for:	used for:
– paying wages	– power bills	– loan repayments
– paying suppliers	– insurance premiums	– mortgage payments

Faster Payments Service

- a bank-to-bank **electronic** transfer system which enables customers to send payments to other bank accounts
- telephoned or online instructions accepted for immediate or future payments
- money transfer time **no more than two hours**
- intended for **small or medium-sized amounts**, maximum £100,000

CHAPS (Clearing House Automated Payments Services)

- a bank-to-bank **electronic** transfer system
- **same day** irrevocable payments (ie cannot be cancelled)
- used for **high value** business-to-business payments, all types of property purchase

bank draft

- a **paper-based** transfer – a bank draft is a **bank cheque** (ie written out by a bank)
- a **high-value** transfer – guaranteed payment to the person receiving it
- used for **large purchases** where payment has to be guaranteed – eg car purchase

payment type	format	how it works	clearing time
cheque	paper	sent to bank of issuer for payment, can be stopped	3 days
bank giro credit	paper	paid into bank with cash or cheques, used for bills	3 days
debit card	plastic	money deducted direct from customer's account	1-2 days
credit card	plastic	credit account settled monthly	30 days
BACS direct credit	electronic	bulk payments, eg wages	3 days
BACS direct debit	electronic	set up by business being paid, variable amounts and dates	3 days
BACS standing order	electronic	set up by person paying fixed amounts and dates	3 days
Faster Payments Service	electronic	set up by person paying	up to 2 hours
CHAPS	electronic	very large payments	same day
bank draft	paper	bank cheque – for large payments	3 days

authorising incoming payments

Businesses receive incoming payments in many different formats. Normally, if the payment received is electronic, it can be assumed that it is correct and will not be refused by the bank of the person paying.

But there are situations where incoming payments will need to be checked or authorised. These include cheques, debit cards and credit cards.

checking cheques

- the cheque must be signed – it is completely invalid if it is not
- the name of the payee (person receiving the cheque) must be present and correct
- the amount in words and figures must be the same
- the date must be present and the cheque must be in date, ie no more than six months old (note that if the date is missing the payee can write it in)

If anything is wrong with the cheque (apart from a missing date) it <u>must</u> be returned to the issuer.

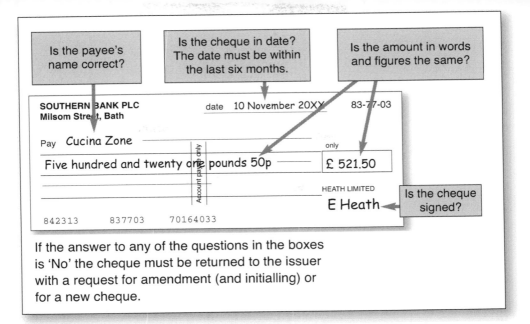

Is the payee's name correct?

Is the cheque in date? The date must be within the last six months.

Is the amount in words and figures the same?

SOUTHERN BANK PLC
Milsom Street, Bath

date 10 November 20XX   83-77-03

Pay Cucina Zone   only

Five hundred and twenty one pounds 50p   £ 521.50

Account payee only

HEATH LIMITED

E Heath

Is the cheque signed?

842313   837703   70164033

If the answer to any of the questions in the boxes is 'No' the cheque must be returned to the issuer with a request for amendment (and initialling) or for a new cheque.

checking payments made by debit and credit card

Debit and credit card payments are increasingly being used for making payment for goods and services. This can happen in two situations:

- when a **customer is present**, eg in a shop, where 'chip and PIN' is used and a 4 digit PIN (Personal Identification Number) is entered by the customer
- when a **customer is not present**, eg in an online purchase, when a range of details has to be provided by the customer

In both cases the organisation taking payment must ensure that a set procedure is followed and the necessary details obtained.

payments made by debit and credit card – customer present

- details of the transaction are entered on the online till or handheld terminal
- the customer confirms the details are correct
- the customer enters his or her PIN number
- the payment is then either accepted or rejected (for example, the payment may be refused if the cardholder has not got the funds, or if the card is stolen)
- the money is taken direct from the account of the card-holder – a **guaranteed payment**

payments made by debit and credit card – customer not present

- the transaction may take place by mail-order, online or over the telephone, using a debit card or a credit card

- as the customer is not present, 'chip and PIN' cannot be used

- the following details will be needed by the seller:

    - the card number, three digit security code and expiry date

    - if it is a debit card, the issue number and/or start date

    - the full name of the cardholder as shown on the card

    - the cardholder's address

    - the cardholder's signature (if mail order is being used)

- as the customer is not present, **payment is not necessarily guaranteed** – the cardholder can ask for a **chargeback** (refund)

    - if the goods are faulty or incorrect

    - if the purchase has been made fraudulently by someone other than the cardholder

13 Bank reconciliation statement

RECONCILING THE BANK STATEMENT AND CASH BOOK

A bank reconciliation statement sets out a calculation which explains the differences between a bank statement final balance and the final balance of the Bank account in the cash book. Bank reconciliation is a fiddly area to deal with and it is important to appreciate the effect of the differences that can occur.

where do you start?

One of the problems encountered is knowing where to start. A common method is to start with the bank statement final balance and move towards the Bank account balance in the cash book. This is done by recording the adjustments in a bank reconciliation statement:

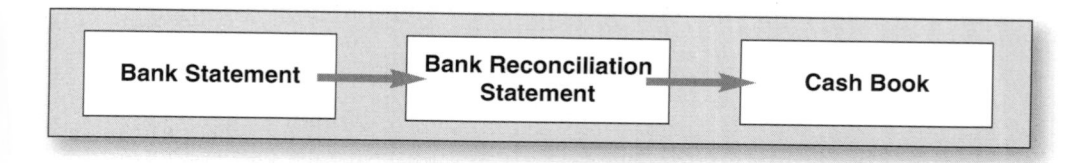

A summary of the calculation, with sample figures, looks like this:

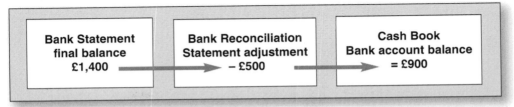

| Bank Statement final balance £1,400 | → | Bank Reconciliation Statement adjustment − £500 | → | Cash Book Bank account balance = £900 |

the process for identifying differences

When you receive the bank statement you should carry out a ticking exercise which will identify any differences between the bank statement and the cash book entries.

■ Tick off the items that are in the bank statement and also in the cash book bank columns. This will mean that you will most likely end up with unticked items in both the bank statement and the cash book.

■ Update the cash book columns with the **unticked** items on the bank statement. These can include a variety of entries, eg bank charges and bank interest. You will need to be familiar with bank statements to know what the entries are. If in doubt, look at the bank statement on the next page and read the explanations that follow.

BANK STATEMENT

Date	Details		Debit	Credit	Balance
20XX					
1 May	Balance				9,881.60
6 May	J Macmillan Ltd	BACS		561.60	10,443.20
10 May	683002	CHO	115.44		10,327.76
13 May	AWA Finance	SO	360.00		9,967.76
17 May	Astley Insurance	DD	98.00		9,869.76
17 May	Doolittle & Daily	CHAPS	8,000.00		1,869.76

TAKE CARE!
on a bank statement a payment out is a **debit** and a payment in is a **credit** - the opposite way round to a cash book!

payment descriptions

BACS	computer transfer between bank accounts (Bankers Automated Clearing Services)
CHO	cheque (the cheque number is in the 'details' column)
SO	Standing Order - computer bank transfer set up by person paying the money
DD	Direct Debit - computer bank transfer set up by business receiving money
CHAPS	Large amount same day bank computer transfer, often used by solicitors

updating the cash book entries

As you can see there are a number of possible unticked items on a bank statement, all of which will need to be entered in the cash book. These are the main ones:

- ■ BACS payments received from customers
- ■ standing orders and direct debits paid out
- ■ CHAPS payments out

Here are some other possibilities (not shown on the bank statement above):

- ■ BACS payments sent to suppliers and BACS payments for wages
- ■ bank charges and bank interest (paid or received)
- ■ dishonoured (unpaid) cheques

final cash book bank balance

When you have completed the update of the Bank account in the cash book you should **balance the bank columns** to extract a final cash book balance.

This is the figure that will be inserted at the end of the Bank Reconciliation Statement.

dealing with the unticked items in the cash book

The differences that are now left between bank statement and cash book (assuming there are no errors) are the **unticked items in the cash book**. These are all **timing differences**:

unpresented cheques

These are cheques issued to suppliers or for other expenses; they have been written into the cash book but have not yet been deducted from the Bank account, and so are not on the bank statement.

outstanding lodgements

An old-fashioned way of describing money which is to be paid into the bank; it has been entered into the cash book but is not yet on the bank statement.

It is these items – the timing differences – which are entered into the Bank Reconciliation Statement to account for the difference between the final balances of the bank statement and updated cash book bank columns.

Study the sample bank reconciliation statement on the next page.

Bank Reconciliation Statement format

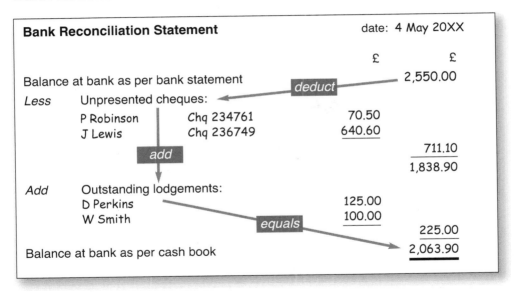

Bank Reconciliation Statement		date: 4 May 20XX	
		£	£
Balance at bank as per bank statement	*deduct*		2,550.00
Less Unpresented cheques:			
P Robinson	Chq 234761	70.50	
J Lewis	Chq 236749	640.60	
add			711.10
			1,838.90
Add Outstanding lodgements:			
D Perkins		125.00	
W Smith	*equals*	100.00	
			225.00
Balance at bank as per cash book			2,063.90

the bank reconciliation process at a glance

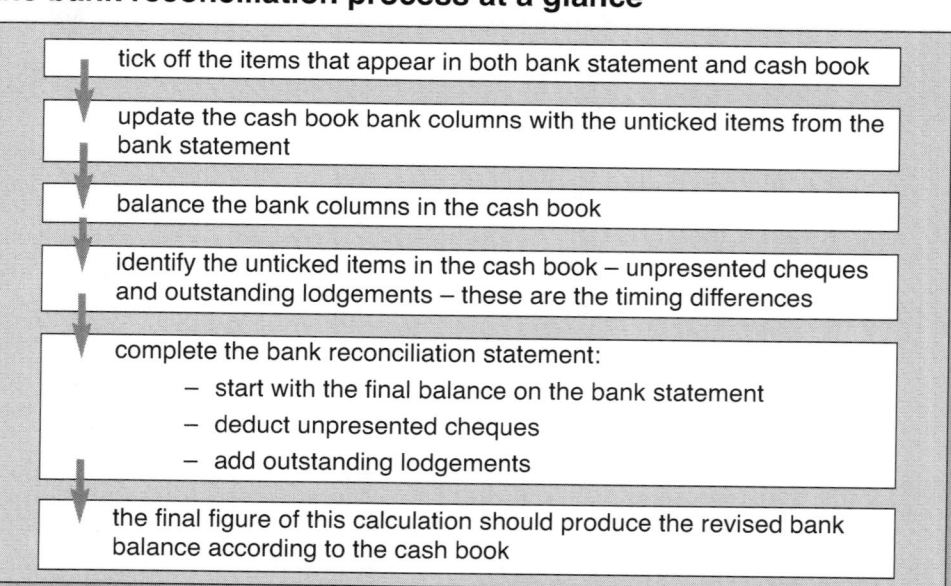

tick off the items that appear in both bank statement and cash book

update the cash book bank columns with the unticked items from the bank statement

balance the bank columns in the cash book

identify the unticked items in the cash book – unpresented cheques and outstanding lodgements – these are the timing differences

complete the bank reconciliation statement:
- start with the final balance on the bank statement
- deduct unpresented cheques
- add outstanding lodgements

the final figure of this calculation should produce the revised bank balance according to the cash book

summary of the completed bank reconciliation documents

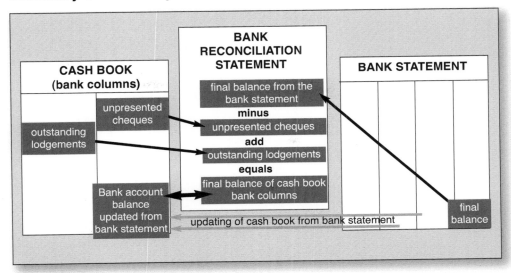

KEEPING YOUR MEMORY FIT

The human brain is an odd organ – you can remember the most useless facts, but when it comes to complex matters such as accounting procedures the mind can go completely blank. But it is possible to train your brain.

At the beginning of this Guide there are some revision tips which suggest that you can study effectively and recall information by . . .

- **Observing**, ie remembering what information looks like on the page, using diagrams, lists, mind-maps and colour coding. Memory is very visual.

- **Writing** information down, using flash cards, post-it notes, notes on a phone. It is the actual process of writing which helps to fix the information in the brain.

- **Learning** by regularly going through your course notes and text books. Find a 'study buddy' in your class (or online) to teach and test each other as the course progresses.

- **Chill out** when you get tired. Give your brain a chance to recover. Get some exercise and fresh air, work out. In the ancient world there was the saying that "a fit body is home to a fit mind."

- **Treats** – promise yourself rewards when you have finished studying – meet friends, eat chocolate, have a drink, listen to music.

exam preparation

- **Practice, practice, practice** when preparing for your assessment.

  Practice the questions and assessments in the Osborne Books workbooks.

  Practice the free online assessments on the Osborne Books website:

  Log on to www.osbornebooks.co.uk/elearning or scan this . . .

some aids to memory

On the next few pages are blank spaces for you to set out ways of remembering

- the formula for working out the VAT contained in a gross amount which already includes VAT

- the debit and credit entries which are contained in the control accounts

formula for calculating VAT content of VAT-inclusive amount . . .

example calculation

Write the names of the accounts on the correct sides of the control account.

debits	SALES LEDGER CONTROL ACCOUNT	credits

Write the names of the accounts on the correct sides of the control account.

debits	PURCHASES LEDGER CONTROL ACCOUNT	credits

Write the names of the accounts on the correct sides of the VAT account.

debits	VAT CONTROL ACCOUNT	credits